T0197489

# A Psalm A Day

Words of spiritual healing & inspiration

FRANCES ARRINGTON

Scripture quotations marked KJV are from the Holy Bible,
King James Version (Authorized Version). First published
in 1611. Quoted from the KJV Classic Reference Bible,
Copyright © 1983 by The Zondervan Corporation.

To order additional copies of this book, contact:
Xlibris
844-714-8691
www.Xlibris.com
Orders@Xlibris.com

ISBN:   Softcover        978-1-6698-1585-3
        EBook            978-1-6698-1584-6

Print information available on the last page

Rev. date: 03/14/2022

# Dedication

*To my mother, Clara H. Mann, who always found a way to indulge the wide-eyed dreams of her youngest daughter.*

# Introduction

In the Holy Bible, the Book of Psalms was written by King David. The psalms are both lyrical and historical, documenting much of King David's life. The story of King David figures very prominently in the Holy Bible, from his triumph over Goliath to his rise to the throne of Israel. The psalms are in fact poems, written to be put to music with the help of harps, lyres and other instruments prevalent in his day. In fact, many of the psalms include instructions from King David to the musicians who would perform them at celebrations and other momentous occasions.

# Foreword

Throughout my own life, I have found comfort in the Book of Psalms. Among my favorites are Psalm 27 and Psalm 91. They are among those that I am sharing in this book. The life of King David is bittersweet, full of great highs and devastating lows. As many writers do, he seemed to find some relief in sharing the good and the bad with others through the written word. He also left his writings open for musical interpretation. The psalms touch upon some very difficult and complicated times, yet they are simply written and easily understood. Which is the true mark of a great writer.

# Meditations

I hope that the excerpts that I have shared here from the Book of Psalms will bring you some comfort and lead you to explore these passages for yourself. You may find them appealing for entirely different reasons than why I find them appealing. The photographs are all mine, taken in different locations and on different occasions. The beaches are either in my home state of North Carolina or in Virginia. I love the outdoors. I find great comfort in peaceful meditations of a sunrise, sunset, flowers, and of course beaches. I left some blank pages at the end of the book for you to make your own notes. Enjoy.

*I will say of the Lord, He is my refuge and my fortress: my God: in Him will I trust.*

*Psalm 91*

# A Psalm A Day

Trust means different things to different people. Few relationships survive or thrive without trust. In our secular relationships, we expect others to do what they say they are going to do, to keep their word. We expect them to be there when we need them and they expect that same reliability from us. When those levels of trust are violated, relationships are damaged, sometimes irreparably. We are blessed that our trust in God brings with it greater levels of expectation. We know that He will be there in our times of need. He is a refuge, a place to run to when we feel lost, afraid or alone. His love for us is everlasting, ever present. We can trust in that.

Psalm 91: In Him Will I Trust

I have set the Lord always before me:

because he is my right hand, I shall not be moved.

Psalms 16

# A Psalm A Day

I must confess that I have not always consulted the Lord in my decision-making. I have very often consulted my friends, my family, and my colleagues for advice. As I get older, however, I find that I am so glad that I have found this scripture. It exemplifies what I love so much about the Psalms. They are for everyday living! I only wish I had stumbled upon this one in my 20s, 30s, or 40s! It is a reminder that we do have a forever friend in the Lord. It is such a comfort to know that once we choose to set Him before us in our comings and our goings, God is a willing guide to help us navigate life's ups and downs.

Psalm 16: I have set the Lord before me

By the word of the Lord were the heavens made
And all the host of them by the breath of His mouth.

Psalm 33:6

## A Psalm A Day

The photographs and the psalms in this book work together. I chose the photographs to illuminate the words of the psalms. I hope the words of the psalms illuminate the photographs as well. Words have power, especially those in the Book of Psalms. King David chose his words carefully. God is also careful with words. With words He spoke the heavens into existence. On my daily walks, it seemed that I noticed something new in the creation, the flowering of trees, the light shining through, the breeze, the sounds. All Amazing. Do you think that God stood there for just a moment and meditated on the beauty He had just created ?

Psalm 33: By His word were the heavens made.

He leadeth me beside the still waters.

He restoreth my soul.

Psalm 23

Among my favorite places in the world are the beaches along the Outer Banks in North Carolina. The photograph on the prior page was taken during a walk on the beach in Kill Devil Hills. You can see the sun glistening across the water. Imagine the chill and the breeze. Imagine the comforting sound of water rushing towards the sand which was cold that evening and damp. I understand why David wrote, 'He leads me beside the still waters. He restores my soul.' There is a silence on the water when it is still. The mind calms down. Thinking of only good things. Or of nothing at all.

Psalm 23: Beside the still waters.

My foot standeth in an even place:
in the congregation will I bless the Lord.

Psalm 26

## A Psalm A Day

Take a moment and think about a time when your footing was shaky. Perhaps, your shoes did not fit properly. Or the ground was rocky. Or you missed a step on the stairway. The unsteadiness is worrisome. Who wants to take a fall? I love that photograph of toes in the sand. The sand was cool but dry. My footing was very firm. Only when I walked on the beach where the sand was soaked did my feet sink. David understands the need for sure footing. He says that even place that we seek can be found in the congregation of the Lord. It can be found in our praise, and in our blessing of the Lord.

Psalm 26: In an even place.

*Thy will show me the path of life: in thy presence is fullness of joy.*
*Psalm 16*

## A Psalm A Day

A seat by the water is a sacred place to me. I have driven miles just to sit by a certain river, beach or waterfront. Some people play in the soil of a garden. Some find solace browsing the books in a library. For me, the water's edge is where I clear my head. I have made many important decisions sitting on a gazebo, in a car or on a bench by the water, watching the waves roll by. Should I leave this job? Should I stay in this relationship? Whose report will I believe, God's or the doctors'? Beside the water is a good place to talk with God. He listens there. And if you stay and listen quietly, He will answer.

Psalm 16: The path of life.

From the ends of the earth will I cry unto thee.
For thou hast been a shelter for me; and a
strong tower from the enemy.
Psalm 61

# A Psalm A Day

Has the Lord ever been your only shelter? Has He ever been your only safe place or refuge from those who would do you harm? If so, you understand this psalm. King David knew God this way. Before becoming King, he faced a formidable foe in the giant Goliath. David was just a boy and the odds were very much against him. But God was his refuge, the only defender he would need to be victorious. In our lives, there will be times when we face obstacles that seem insurmountable. It may be a person or a predicament. Yet, we can rest easily knowing that we have an advocate in the Lord. From the ends of the earth, He will answer our cries.

Psalm 61: From the ends of the earth.

He gathereth the waters of the sea together as an
heap: he layeth up the depth in storehouses.
Psalms: 33.7

The psalmist writes that the Lord gathers the waters of the sea and places them into storehouses. The idea that the Lord is able to bring together the waters of the sea is both fascinating and comforting. If you have ever stood next to a large body of water and watched as its waves move off into the distance, then you know how vast the waters are. Who can measure how wide or how deep an ocean or river is? Yet, King David says that the Lord is indeed able to gather up the waters and put them into storehouses. Whose storehouses could contain the waters in their awesomeness? Only the Lord in his magnificence could perform it.

Psalm 33: The waters of the sea.

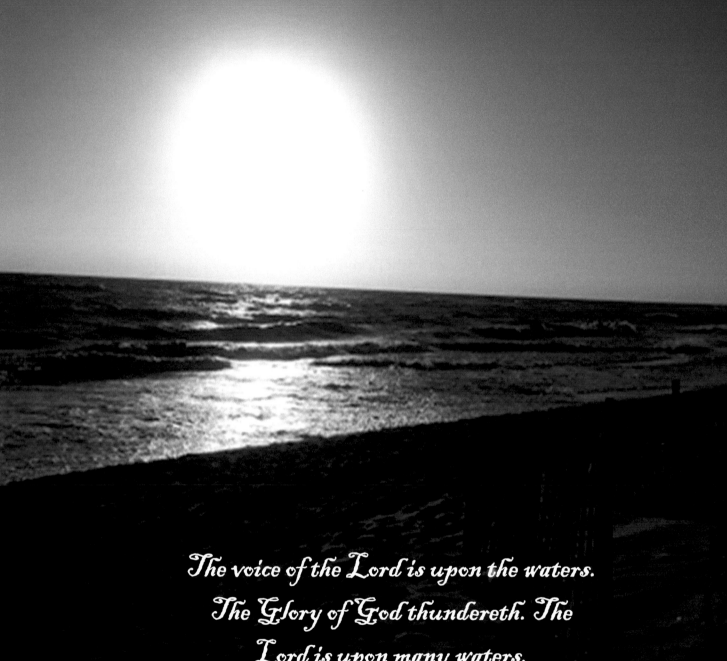

*The voice of the Lord is upon the waters.*
*The Glory of God thundereth. The*
*Lord is upon many waters.*
*Psalm 29*

I take great comfort in watching the waves of a body of water move along. Waves seem to move at their own pace and towards their own destination. Watching from the shore of a beach, waves seem silent, growing louder as they get closer. I have sat beside lakes, beaches, oceans and ponds. If I get very quiet and sit very still, there is a certain sound that comes off the water that is difficult to describe. It is strong, and powerful, and soothing. It is not surprising that the psalmist says the voice of the Lord is upon the waters. That it is like thunder over many waters. Listen next time you are near the water. Listen for the voice of the Lord.

Psalm 29: The voice of the Lord.

The Lord is my light and my salvation.
Whom shall I fear? The Lord is the strength of my life.
Of whom shall I be afraid?

Psalm 27

# A Psalm A Day

King David was not a perfect man. His life was not one of moral piety. He loved Bathsheba and led her husband into mortal combat to have her for himself. He had many enemies. He faced many trials. But his life was anointed by God. In his youth, he had slain the giant Goliath to save his people. He rose to the throne of Israel and ruled for many years. He was never too proud to acknowledge his wrongdoings before God. So, he enjoyed the favor of God. He knew God's love, His wrath and His forgiveness. God was his protector and savior. In God, he knew he had nothing to fear. The Book of Psalms expresses his gratitude and his humility.

Psalm 27: Whom shall I fear?

Bless the Lord, O my soul, and
forget not all his benefits.
Psalm 103

# A Psalm A Day

This is one of my favorite psalms. Primarily, because we as believers are called to 'Bless the Lord'. We are usually seeking blessings from God. Our requests may be related to health, finances, family or work. We each face our own challenges in life. We are in all need of His blessings. And, as the psalmist writes, many are our benefits as believers. Yet, David tells his soul to bless the Lord. How do you bless the Lord? How does one bless an Almighty, All-Knowing, and Ever-Present God? In prayers for His prosperity, His strength, and His sovereignty? In praise of His creation? In humble expressions of love, gratitude, and honor, I bless the Lord.

Psalm 103: Bless the Lord, O my soul.

Wait on the Lord, be of good courage, and
he shall strengthen thine heart.
Psalm 27

I do not like to wait. I have plans. I prefer to be organized at home, in my work life, and right now in university studies. Patience is a virtue that I continue to learn. This psalm has a particular goal. David is encouraging himself. He is expecting God to strengthen his heart, to provide him courage no doubt to get through some challenge in his life. This is what I love about the Book of Psalms, they are meant to help us get through the challenges of everyday life. Who has not at some point faced a challenge that shook your courage, that weakened your heart? Who has not wondered will I make it through this? This is your psalm. Wait on the Lord.

Psalm 27: Wait on the Lord.

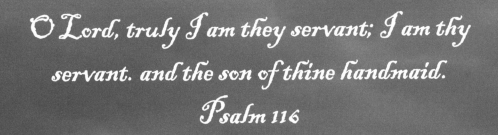

O Lord, truly I am they servant; I am thy servant. and the son of thine handmaid.
Psalm 116

I wanted a special psalm to close out the book. I wanted one that would resonate with you, that would give you something to think about. Do you call yourself a servant of the Lord? I do. I often say to God, in the conversational tone that I use to talk to God, that I am doing this or that 'in your service' or 'if it is your will'. This does not mean that I never fall short. I do. Often. I trust God to forgive me for those times. One message rings true throughout the Book of Psalms, and is especially true in King David's life, is that he is a man of human weaknesses. Yet, he is a man who is loved by God. He is a servant of God. Are you a servant of God?

Psalm 116: I am thy servant.

Notes:

## Notes:

## Notes:

## Notes:

Printed in the United States
by Baker & Taylor Publisher Services